# THE
# BROOKLYN
## TRIVIA BOOK

### DAVID A. WEISS

Order this book online at www.trafford.com
or email orders@trafford.com

Most Trafford titles are also available at major online book retailers.

Print information available on the last page.

Library of Congress Control Number: 2017912105

ISBN: 978-1-4907-8393-2 (sc)
ISBN: 978-1-4907-8395-6 (hc)
ISBN: 978-1-4907-8394-9 (e)

*Trafford rev. 09/18/2017*

 www.trafford.com

**North America & international**
toll-free: 1 888 232 4444 (USA & Canada)
fax: 812 355 4082

I would be amiss if I didn't acknowledge that through the years I have received the help and support from a special group of friends. Their names are Walter Freeman, Irving smith Kogan, Philip Gerard, Henrik Grogius and Chris Davis.

It has been said that seven in every ten Americans have a link to Brooklyn.

Although there are several explanations as to how Brooklyn got the name *Brooklyn*, the one accepted by most historians is that the terrain reminded the early settlers of a small town outside Amsterdam called Breuckelen—a name that, through the years, evolved into *Brooklyn*.

Like its American counterpart, Breuckelen remained independent for hundreds of years, not being taken over by Amsterdam until the twenty-first century.

The first European to reach Brooklyn from Europe was Giovanni Verrazano in 1503, and not many people believe that it was not until Henry Hudson came a century later in 1632 that the next European came.

If you want to know why Henry Hudson sailed under the Dutch West India Company flag instead of the flag of his native England, it was because two of his previous voyages—which had been done for English backers—had ended in failure, and he could get backing nowhere else.

Not all Brooklynites were in favor of consolidating with Manhattan and the other boroughs in 1898. A nonbinding poll taken several years before showed the vote for consolidation was whisper thin, but Brooklyn (along with East Bronx, Queens, and Staten Island) was united with Manhattan to form Greater New York in 1898. All were not happy though, and in 1915, a bill was introduced in the state legislature to correct the terrible mistake and return Brooklyn to an independent entity. It failed.

What most Brooklynites don't know is that it was the Lenape Indian tribe from Brooklyn—and not an Indian tribe from Manhattan—who sold Manhattan to the Dutch for twenty-four dollars.

The longest street in Brooklyn is Bedford Avenue, which stretches 10.1 miles from Greenpoint to Sheepshead Bay.

It was a pitcher for the Brooklyn Excelsiors named Arthur William "Candy" Cummings who made professional baseball the sport it is today by inventing the curveball in the 1860s. He said he got the idea for it by watching the gyrations of seashells that he tossed in the ocean.

Although there are only Seven Wonders of the World, the Brooklyn Bridge is often referred to as the "Eighth Wonder of the World."

Strangely, even though there are dozens of streets in Brooklyn named for nonentities, there is not one street named for the Brooklyn minister Henry Ward Beecher, who was considered the most popular man in the United States throughout much of the nineteenth century.

Did you know that the "population" of Brooklyn's Green-Wood Cemetery is not much different than the population of Boston, Massachusetts?

By a strange coincidence, the last movie shown at the RKO Albee in Downtown Brooklyn—the year was 1978—was a screen version of the play *Who's Afraid of Virginia Woolf?* It was written by Edward Albee, adopted grandson of B. F. Albee, the vaudeville magnate who had built the theater and named it after himself.

The only readable grave in the Montauket Indian cemetery on Long Island is that of Stephen Talkhouse, who, during his adult lifetime, walked regularly every day, back and forth from Montauk to Easthampton and Southampton.

Yes, it's true. There is a cigarette brand sold worldwide (online in the US) called Peter Stuyvesant Red King, known familiarly as Stuyes. It is promoted as containing "premium tobacco for experienced smokers" and is particularly popular in South Africa, Greece, and Australia.

The only poem of Walt Whitman to be published during his lifetime was "O Captain, My Captain" in an anthology, the ode he wrote on the death of Abraham Lincoln.

The Gerritsen family deserves special mention in Brooklyn's Hall of Fame. Not only did they build North America's first tide-powered gristmill in the mid-1660s, but they also operated it continuously for almost three centuries until an arson-set fire destroyed the mill in 1934.

Are those who reside in Cobble Hill aware that Cobble Hill Park's current location was the site of Brooklyn's Second Unitarian Church, affectionately called Church of the Turtle because of its shape? Its first minister was Samuel Longfellow, brother of the poet Henry Wadsworth Longfellow.

One of the names used for the Williamsburg Bridge before it officially became the Williamsburg Bridge was the East River Bridge.

The one man from Brooklyn closest to becoming president of the United States was Henry Cruse Murphy who, in the nineteenth century, was a New York State senator, publisher of the *Brooklyn Eagle*, mayor of Brooklyn (when he was only thirty-one years old), and two-term US congressman, among other things. In 1852 he came close to getting the nomination of the Democratic candidate for the presidency, losing out by only one vote to Franklin Pierce who became the nominee that year and went on to win the nomination and later the presidency in the general election.

There is a footnote to history in St. Mary's Star of the Sea Church at 467 Court Street in Cobble Hill. It was here that Al Capone—born and raised in Brooklyn before he went to Chicago and became famous as the nation's number 1 gangster—married a beautiful Irish girl named Mae Coughlin.

Not everyone was thrilled to hear Brooklyn's famous minister Henry Ward Beecher preach. Like all famous men, he had his detractors, such as one who called him the Gospel of Gush or another who complained that he screeched instead of preached.

According to one account, the number of soldiers contributed by Brooklyn to the armed services in

World War II was greater than the total contributed by thirty-eight different US states.

Don't think that William M. "Boss" Tweed was all bad, even though at taxpayer expense he accumulated a fortune estimated to total $200 million through fraud and kickbacks. Among other things, he founded the Manhattan Eye and Ear Hospital, raised funds for orphanages and public baths, fought to get the land the American Museum of Natural History was built on, and most importantly, was the man the city fathers of Brooklyn hired to lobby before the New York State Legislature to get the initial funds to start building the Brooklyn Bridge.

The last Brooklyn Dodger to retire from the Los Angeles Dodgers was Don Drysdale in 1969.

Some of the inhabitants of Sheepshead Bay are descendants of the stableboys and jockeys who once worked at the old Sheepshead Bay racetrack.

Did you know there are twenty miles of paths and roads in Green-Wood Cemetery?

In 1834, Brooklyn, then an independent city, became the third leading city in the United

States in terms of population—a ranking it held throughout most of the nineteenth century.

Although tourist guides and guidebooks often point out that the Commandant's House at the Brooklyn Navy Yard was possibly designed by Charles Bulfinch, the architect for part of the US Capitol Building, today's historians seriously doubt that, saying the Bulfinch connection was more likely "a fantasy of nineteenth-century writers."

In retrospect, the great achievement of Brooklyn-born William Van Alen, who was the chief architect of the Chrysler Building, was a mixed blessing. When he submitted the bill for his services, Walter Chrysler refused to pay the amount on the grounds they had no written agreement, and Van Alen had to sue to get his money. He won the suit, but the fact he had to litigate to get it turned off any chance of future assignments. He ended up a teacher of sculpture.

Although Fort Hamilton was obviously named for Alexander Hamilton, no contemporary account exists as to how and when this came about.

Not all the famous celebrities buried in Brooklyn are in Green-Wood Cemetery. For example, in Cypress Hills Cemetery, which is on the

Brooklyn-Queens border, are the graves of Jackie Robinson, Mae West, Eubie Blake, and the Collyer brothers.

The people of Baltimore are rightly proud of the running of the Preakness Stakes—the second race in the Triple Crown—at the city's Pimlico Race Course. But do they know that from 1890 to 1904, the Preakness was run at the Gravesend racetrack in Coney Island?

In the 1920s, there was a plan that seemed a fait accompli to eliminate King's Highway; but at the last minute, the city fathers not only reversed themselves and left it standing, but also widened its streets.

An unsung Brooklyn hero was Cyrus Smith, a mayor of Brooklyn in the early nineteenth century when it was the third largest city in the United States. Trying to establish Brooklyn's first public hospital, he went to the Board of Aldermen to get financing. When it offered him only $200, he sold his own house to obtain the funds to build it, and that, according to one account, was the beginning of what is now today's Brooklyn Hospital.

Try to find the beach when you go to the Bath Beach section of Brooklyn. There has been no direct access to the beach since Shore Road was constructed by Robert Moses in the 1950s.

As they say, there is nothing new under the sun. That floating swimming pool the New York City Parks Department moored several years ago in the East River opposite Brooklyn Heights was not the first floating swimming pool to be anchored there. A century and a half previously, there was a floating covered barge called Gray's Baths tied up in almost the very same spot. One famous person who wrote about swimming there was Walt Whitman.

One of the biggest expenses the city of Brooklyn incurred in 1863 was paying the $300,000 bounty to the men who volunteered for service in the Union Army. To meet the demand, the city had to obtain a special loan of $250,000.

In the War of 1812, Brooklyn got a scare when it was reported that a British fleet was spotted off Sandy Hook. The entire population, young and old, pitched in building fortifications along the shore, but the fleet, for reasons unknown, never did attack.

It was not only the famous saltwater pool of the St. George Hotel that was so spectacular. So was the grand ballroom above the pool. Said to be the largest hotel ballroom in the world, it measured 130 times 116 square feet and featured a device called Colorama that produced a changing sequence of colors and shadows via twelve thousand colored electric light bulbs.

Robert Fulton didn't forget his employees on the *Nassau*, the ferry that, in 1814, launched ferry service between New York and Brooklyn. Years after one employee had retired, he could still be seen at one end of the *Nassau*, where he had been given space to sell cookies and candies to the passengers.

It was Brooklyn's Charles Ebbets, head of the Dodgers for many years, who invented the rain check now standard at all major-league ballparks.

Many people assume it was William Wrigley Jr. who introduced the first commercially made chewing gum in the United States. It was actually a Brooklyn inventor named Thomas Adams, and—believe it or not—he got the idea from General Antonio Lopez de Santa Anna, the infamous conqueror of the Alamo who, after being sent in exile, lived briefly in Staten Island. Showing Adams some samples of chicle, which he had brought from his homeland to chew on, Santa Anna suggested the chicle might have potential as a substitute for rubber and suggested that Adams try to see if he could do something with it. Adams tried to make toys from it and also used it as tires on wagon wheels; and when all that didn't pan out, he formed it into sticks, which he began to market as chewing gum. His company, which he established on Sands Street in 1861, is still a factor in the chewing gum market, having introduced such popular brands as Black Jack and Chiclets through the years.

In the first St. Ann's Episcopal Church, which stood at the corner of Sands and Washington streets, there were two columns of listings for the baptisms of African Americans. One column had the heading *Black*; the other, the heading *Free Black*.

If you are a baseball fan, you might like to know that at 133 Clinton Street, there is a plaque on the exterior of the brick building announcing that the building was once the clubhouse of the Brooklyn Excelsiors, a famous nineteenth-century baseball team.

All that is left of the Brooklyn's original Hall of Records, which was located on Joralemon Street across Brooklyn's Borough Hall, are two outdoor lighting standards that have been reinstalled at the southern entrance to the New York State Supreme Court on Cadman Plaza East.

Yes, there really was a hill in Cobble Hill, and it played an important role in the Battle of Brooklyn in the American Revolution. At the beginning of the battle, it was from this hill that a small detachment of Continental soldiers stationed there fired two-gun salutes to inform General George Washington that British troops under General Howe had crossed over from Staten Island and were moving into Gravesend. Later, Washington used the hill as a vantage point to view the progress of the battle. After the British occupied Brooklyn, they leveled the hill.

When the Brooklyn Bridge opened in 1883, it was the world's largest leap across space, i.e., 1,595.5 feet.

The longshoremen of Brooklyn showed their true colors when, in the midst of a widespread longshoreman's strike after World War II that affected shipping up and down the entire East Coast, they continued to handle the coffins of GIs being shipped back from Europe at the Brooklyn Army Terminal.

The present headquarters of the Brooklyn Historical Society on Pierrepont Street is not the first building the organization had. When it opened in 1863 as the Long Island Historical Society, its headquarters was at 44 Court Street, where the Temple Bar building is now.

In its 2015 reemergence as a performance theater, the Kings Theater in Flatbush (formerly Loew's Kings) can no longer say it was a "Wonder theater," a claim that everyone assumed referred to the lavishness of its décor when in actuality it meant it had a Wonder organ.

Although several Brooklyn neighborhoods from Brooklyn Heights to Clinton Hill have been singled out at various times as elite places to live, that honor—it may come as a surprise—once applied to Flatbush. In a 1908 book titled *The Realm of Light and Air in the Flatbush of Today*, the author described Flatbush as follows: "Flatbush is the city of beautiful streets, handsome homes, and impressive buildings and is recognized as the most attractive place for residence in the great city of New York."

A real stranger-than-fiction story associated with Green-Wood Cemetery is that of the side-by-side graves of the two Prentiss brothers—one of Clifton Prentiss, who served in the Union Army, and the other of William Prentiss, who was a soldier in the Confederate Army. The story doesn't end here. It seems that in April 1865, they were both mortally wounded in the same battle just a few feet from each other; Clifton was leading an attack on fortified earthworks that William was helping to defend.

The street we know now as Old Fulton Street has gone through three name changes through the years. Before its present name, it was Cadman Plaza East, and before that, it was Fulton Street. Then there was its original name—Ferry Street.

From a safety point of view, it was a good thing the early Brooklyn major-league baseball teams stopped playing at Washington Park in Park Slope. Being made of wood, it was a firetrap.

In 1907 Harry Houdini, the famous magician, introduced one of his most popular escapes in the Orpheum Theater in Downtown Brooklyn. As described in the *Brooklyn Eagle*, "he was able to release himself after being handcuffed and shackled to the four wheels of a large automobile."

A major factor in the growth of Coney Island in the early twentieth century was the support of two brothers from Cleveland, Ohio, named Johnson. The older one, Thomas L. Johnson, had been Cleveland's mayor and a US senator who had become wealthy by inventing the trolley cashbox.

The Johnson brothers set up trolley lines in half a dozen American cities, including Brooklyn where their lines started in different parts of the city and ended up in Coney Island. While here, they lived briefly on Shore Road, and both brothers are buried in Green-Wood Cemetery.

In 1865 when the city of Brooklyn switched over to paid firemen, many of the volunteer fire organizations reorganized themselves as veterans' organizations and for years afterward, staged parades, fancy balls, and conventions, as they had done previously.

The name of Remsen, one of the first families in Brooklyn Heights, derived from the fact that the original name was Rem. And the *sen* part, which came later, brought the name to mean "son of Rem."

One of the names used for the Williamsburg Bridge before it officially became the Williamsburg Bridge was the "East River Bridge."

Did you know the High Street stop in the Independent Subway line is not on High Street but on Cadman Plaza East?

Charles Carroll of Carrollton, the prominent Marylander who was responsible for sending Maryland troops to help out Washington in the Battle of Brooklyn, was distinguished in three other ways besides helping out in the Battle of Brooklyn. First, he was the only Catholic to sign the Declaration of Independence. Second, he also happened to be the last survivor among the signers, not dying until 1832. Third, he was the richest man in the American colonies.

The Brooklyn Museum has another "first" besides being the first children's museum in the United States. As a result of a 2007 renovation, it became the first museum in New York City to be heated and cooled by geothermal wells.

If you are asked how many subway stations there are in New York City, you can give any one of two answers and be correct. The official number is 468; but if you count the stations where there are transfers, the number drops to 423.

Lady Mary Wortley Montagu (no *e*) didn't get into all the encyclopedias because Montague Street in Brooklyn Heights was named for her. Rather, it is because she is considered one of the finest letter-writers in English literature, her correspondents including everyone from Hugh Walpole to

Alexander Pope. Her connection with Brooklyn's Pierrepont family (which gave her name to the street) was that her maiden name was Pierrepont and she was one of their cousins.

There was once a hotel on Fifth Avenue near Flatbush Avenue called the Burton Hotel, which had two distinctions. First, it catered only to men. Second, one of its entrances had swinging doors, like the saloons in the old Wild West.

When Long Island College Hospital set up Brooklyn's first ambulance service in the late nineteenth century, a surgeon was dispatched with the driver on every call.

The first municipality in New Netherland to receive a charter from the Dutch West India Company was the village of Breuckelen (Brooklyn) in 1646. New Amsterdam (New York) didn't receive its charter until seven years later.

Not all was sweetness and light between Flatbush and Flatlands in colonial Brooklyn. In the early seventeenth century, arbitrators had to be called in to settle the disputes over the boundary between the two settlements.

Did you know that East New York Avenue was originally a plank road that went from Flatbush to the Jamaica Plank Road at Jamaica Avenue?

In his lifetime, Peter Stuyvesant was always referred to, not as Peter Stuyvesant, but as Petras Stuyvesant or Pieter Stuyvesant.

On Third Avenue near the Old Stone House is the oldest section remaining of a major big-league ballpark still standing—i.e., a wall that was the back wall to what was then Washington Park, where the Brooklyn Dodgers and some of Brooklyn's earlier teams, like the Superbas, played before Ebbets Field was built.

It's surprising that Theodore Roosevelt wasn't buried in Green-Wood Cemetery in Brooklyn rather than in Oyster Bay, for it was in Green-Wood where not only his mother and father were interred, but also his first wife.

During World War II when the Brooklyn Navy Yard employed over seventy-one thousand men and women, the New York City Housing Authority, in order to provide housing for some of the workers and their families, erected the Fort Greene Houses, some fifty-five brick buildings ranging in height from six to fifteen stories.

His full name was Hans Von Kaltenborn, but he was always known as H. V. Kaltenborn. He was one of radio's first important news commentators. A resident of Brooklyn Heights (he lived for years on Garden Place), he started out as a reporter for the *Brooklyn Eagle*, a newspaper he was associated with for many years. His fame was national because for three decades he was on network radio (both NBC and CBS), covering firsthand news stories from all over the world, from wars like the Spanish Civil War to major political events like the rise of Adolf Hitler. Fluent in three languages, he was one of the first radio commentators to give insights and analysis in addition to straight news, and he never used notes, always speaking extempore.

As Casey Stengel once described Moe Berg, who was signed on by the Brooklyn Robins (later Dodgers) in 1923, saying, "He was the strangest man in baseball." It was not his ball-playing ability that earned him that description, even though he played sixteen years in the major leagues; nor was it the fact that he was fluent in eleven languages, including Japanese. Rather, it was because he was a spy for the US government. In the 1930s, when he went to Japan with an all-star team that included Babe Ruth and Lou Gehrig, he stayed in his Tokyo hotel room; and while they were playing exhibitions, he was taking movies of buildings that were supposedly used later on by General Jimmy Doolittle to identify targets on his historic 1942 World War II bombing mission. Then in World War II, Berg did special assignments for the OSS. He interviewed Tito, the Yugoslavian dictator, to assess his future value to the United States and, posing as a physicist, attended a lecture in Switzerland by Werner Heisenberg, head of Germany's atomic bomb project.

According to the *AIA Guide to New York City*, the two greatest Brooklyn architects were Frank Freeman (the Chase Manhattan Bank, St. Ann and the Holy Trinity, etc.) and Montrose Morris (the Alhambra Apartments, St. George Hotel, etc.)

The Gerritsen family, who operated a mill in what is now Marine Park, established something of a longevity record. Its first mill was established in the 1650s, and not until the 1930s did the family cease its mill operations.

Montague Street in Brooklyn Heights did not become an official New York City street until the 1930s. Unknown to everyone, it had been a private street owned for three centuries by the Pierrepont family who, when they learned of their ownership, sold it to the city.

Two of the top Mafia criminals of the twentieth century were Brooklynites who ended up in Chicago—i.e., John Torrio, whose contribution was to organize the Mafia on a national basis, and Al Capone, his successor, who was the nation's most wanted criminal in the 1920s and 1930s.

Strangely, Henry Ward Beecher, who during his lifetime as head of Brooklyn's Church of the Pilgrims was considered the most popular man in the United States, has not one street in Brooklyn named for him, whereas there are dozens of streets named after nonentities.

If you think Henry Hudson was the first European to set his eyes on Brooklyn, you are mistaken. He arrived in 1632. It was almost a century before— in 1564, to be exact—when Giovanni Verrazano reached our shores.

The success of Charles Pratt, Brooklyn's richest individual for many years, was due not only to Astral Oil, superior kerosene his company marketed, but also to the fact that for more than a decade he had been the secret partner of John D. Rockefeller.

In the publicity surrounding the multimillion restoration of Loew's Theater completed in 2015, it was usually mentioned that it was originally one of five "Wonder theatres" its owner built in the New York metropolitan area. Most people assumed this adjective referred to the theaters' lavish décor, but it actually stood for the fact that the theaters were equipped with Wonder organs.

Anybody remember freewheeling? When I was a kid, that was the buzzword when it came to automobiles, and if you don't believe me, go to the Brooklyn Public Library on Eastern Parkway and look at the auto ads in early 1930s issues of the *Brooklyn Daily Eagle*.

Did you know it was Hezekiah B. Pierrepont who was responsible for the street layout of Brooklyn Heights? Soon after Brooklyn officially became a town in 1816, he succeeded in persuading the authorities to adopt a street plan that his surveyor had prepared.

The present headquarters of the Brooklyn Historical Society on Pierrepont Street is not the first building the organization had. When it opened in 1863 as the Long Island Historical Society, its headquarters was at 44 Court Street, where the Temple Bar building is now.

Newly published is a fascinating book titled *Brooklyn by Name*, which tells how our streets, neighborhoods, parks, etc., got their names. The authors are Leonard Benardo and Jennifer Weiss.

To add insult to injury, after the move of the Brooklyn Dodgers to Los Angeles, it was revealed that Branch Rickey, the Dodger president who engineered the sale, had been in contact with Norris Poulson, the mayor of Los Angeles, for over a year.

If anyone asks you where the famous chase scene in the movie *The French Connection* took place, you can tell them it was along the N subway line near the Stillwell Avenue exit.

Dyker Heights was one of the last areas of Brooklyn to become settled. While other neighborhoods were growing up among Dutch rule in the early colonial days, it remained woodland into the beginning of the nineteenth century because its land was too sloped for farming.

Among the major-league baseball players who started out playing in Prospect Park when they were teenagers were Lee Mazilli, Willie Randolph, Joe Torre, Chuck Connors, Joe Pepitone, and Sandy Koufax.

When Prohibition came, Brooklyn's breweries did everything possible to keep financially afloat. One in Bushwick went to the extent of brewing spruce beer from the leaves and twigs of spruce trees.

When built in 1854, Packer Collegiate Institute was not the first educational institution to be located on Joralemon Street in Brooklyn Heights. The Brooklyn Female Academy, which had been destroyed by fire two years before, used to be on that site.

There are only two other triumphal arches in New York City besides the triumphal arch at the entrance to Brooklyn's Prospect Park—the arch at Washington Square and the arch at the entrance to the Manhattan Bridge.

Supposedly, the entrance to the house at 2 Sidney Place in Brooklyn Heights originally belonged to a house that had been torn down to make room for the Towers Hotel that was being built on Pierrepont Street.

Did you know that the original name of Garfield Place in Park Slope was Macomb Street? The renaming of the street in honor of President Garfield took place in 1881, two years after Garfield's assassination.

Do the residents of 916 President Street in Park Slope know that this was the home of Laura Jean Libbey, a best-selling author of romantic novels in the early 1900s? She wrote more than eighty books in all, with titles like *The Price of a Kiss* and *The Fatal Wooing*.

A major factor in the growth of Coney Island in the early twentieth century was the support of two brothers named Johnson from Cleveland, Ohio, one of whom was Cleveland's mayor. Realizing that transportation was a key factor in developing the area, they built trolley car lines from different parts of Brooklyn to Coney Island. Later on, they supported Charles Ebbets when he built Ebbets Field.

Did you know that there was a landmark police precinct station house in Brooklyn whose building was constructed in 1898 to resemble a medieval castle? It was the 20th Police Precinct Station House and Stable—later the 83rd Precinct Station House— and it is located at 120 Wilson Avenue in Bushwick.

Ironically, Robert Moses—who more than anyone else transformed New York into an automobile city with his roadways, tunnels, and bridges—never had a driver's license and, according to some, did not know how to drive.

Until 1898 when the New York State Legislature approved a bill permitting prizefighting in the state, there were no legal boxing matches in New York. The fights held were either illegal or held on private property.

In case you forgot, Brooklyn's official flower is the forsythia.

The historians at Plymouth Church can tell you exactly where Lincoln sat when he came to Brooklyn in 1860 to hear Reverend Henry Ward Beecher speak, but they cannot tell you where he sat when he came two weeks later. This is because he sat in a numbered pew the first time; the second time, he was in the balcony where the seats were not numbered.

Unlike the other great Coney Island amusement parks—Dreamland and Luna Park—Steeplechase Park had a fence around it. So in the other parks, people could come and go; at Steeplechase Park, once inside they could not get out without going through the main gate.

In a review of the acclaimed novel *Call It Sleep* by Henry Roth, a writer from Brownsville, a book critic wrote, "This book is to Brownsville what *Moby Dick* is to Nantucket."

According to the 1790 US Census, Oyster Bay in Long Island had a larger population than Brooklyn.

If you want to know where many of Brooklyn's earliest settlers and their families are buried, it is in the graveyard of the historic Flatbush Reformed Dutch Church. The names of those whose graves are there include Lefferts, Van Sickelen, Cortelyou, Bergen, Lott, and Vanderbilt.

Of all those who tried to swindle naïve tourists into buying the Brooklyn Bridge, the best known was George Parker, a career criminal who ended up dying in prison in 1928. Through the years, he found victims willing to buy not only the bridge but also the Statue of Liberty, the old Madison Square Garden, and Grant's Tomb where he passed himself off as Grant's grandson.

The original name for Cypress Hills was Union Place, so named for a racetrack there, Union Course Race Track, which attracted visitors from all over the US and about which Oliver Wendell Holmes wrote a poem.

For Brooklyn, 1906 was a banner year. Not only was it the year that trolley cars were introduced, but it was also the year that the Brooklyn Dodgers won their first National League pennant.

An email from my "mystery correspondents" confirms that although the *Hearst* sports cartoonist Tad Durgan probably did not originate *hot dog*, he did create or publicize a dozen other slang expressions that we still use today, such as *drugstore cowboy, dumbbell,* "yes, we have no bananas," "twenty-three Skidoo," and "for crying out loud."

The first artillery barrage in the American Revolution's Battle of Brooklyn took place at Fort Hamilton when the Continental troops fired at the HMS *Asia* as it was conveying British troops from Staten Island to Brooklyn by way of Bay Ridge. Although the gunfire did some damage and chalked up a few casualties, it had virtually no effect on the fifteen thousand British reg and Hessian troops that were moving down into Brooklyn.

Legend has it that Thomas Durant, president of the railroads, was one of the men who hammered the golden spike that inaugurated the nation's first transcontinental railroad connection between the East and West coasts at Promontory Summit, Utah, in 1869. Actually, the golden spikes—there were four in all—were commemorative spikes. The real iron spike that made the connection was supposed to have been driven by Durant and

Leland Stanford, but both men failed to drive it successfully. The actual spike was hammered in by a railroad employee.

The Flatbush Dutch Reform Church on Church Avenue in Flatbush is the third one on the site. The first, which was made of wood and shaped in the form of a rose, was built in 1654. The second church in 1698 was made of Manhattan schist, and the third and current church dates from 1783.

We all know that the Bedford neighborhood, which played such an important part in the early history of Brooklyn because it was on the route from Fulton Ferry to Long Island, was named for the Duke of Bedford. My old encyclopedia lists a dozen Dukes of Bedford, but I suspect the one connected to this Bedford was William Russell, who died in 1700.

When you walk down Fulton Street in Downtown Brooklyn, it's hard to realize that there were once restaurants there to suit every budget and culinary taste—not only Gage and Tollner, but also Schrafft's, Bickford's, Childs, and the Automat.

Although, until recently, the boardwalk at Coney Island was officially known as the Riegelmann Boardwalk (the name it was given in honor of the Brooklyn borough president who had pushed for its construction), it is now officially the Coney Island Boardwalk.

In 1927 when the Brooklyn Botanic Garden started excavating the land for its rose garden, they found an old cobblestone road that no one knew had existed two feet below the surface.

Those wealthy Brooklyn Heightsians who owned mansions on Columbia Heights had more to look at than just the harbor. It seems that planted on the roofs of the piers below at Furman Street were actual gardens of plants, trees, grass, and shrubbery.

With their 12,800 apartments in twenty buildings, the Williamsburg Houses were the largest slum clearance and low-income housing project undertaken by FDR's Federal Housing Program.

I wonder how many residents of Brooklyn Heights know that their neighborhood was known in colonial days as Clover Hill?

Yes, there is a monument to the *Monitor*, the world's first ironclad warship. It's in McGoldrick Park in Greenpoint, where the famous ship was built in the Civil War.

One of Brooklyn's casualties in World War II was the demolition of its original Wallabout Market to make room for the wartime expansion of the Brooklyn Navy Yard. It was the second largest wholesale food market in the world. It had been built in the 1880s on land that had belonged to the Navy Yard, which the US Congress sold to Brooklyn, then an independent city. With architecture reminiscent of Dutch New Amsterdam, it consisted of blocks of two-story brick buildings, each surrounded by a watchtower and weathercock, all grouped around a wide plaza called Farmers' Square, which was filled with stalls. Although it was deserted in the daytime, it came alive from midnight to dawn. According to the *1939 WPA Guide to New York City*, it would be thronged "with a solid mass of vehicles, crates, barrels, truck drivers, jobbers, and farmers."

Did you know that to protect Prospect Park's famous Camperdown Elm from the north winds, several buildings surrounding it were given landmark status?

Do those who live in the upscale gated community of Sea Gate know that before Sea Gate was built, the area was known as Norton's Point, an infamous section of Coney Island with a reputation for gambling, prostitution, and crime?

The oldest known concrete building in New York City is located at the southwest corner of Third Street at 360 Third Avenue in Brooklyn. Originally the headquarters of the New York and Long Island Coignet Stone Co., the company that built the arches for St. Patrick's Cathedral in Manhattan, it is now in such poor repair that the *AIA Guide to New York City* said it is in need of "immediate architectural CPR."

Joshua Loring, who made a fortune in graft as the commissary officer in charge of feeding those thousands of American prisoners holed up on prison ships in Wallabout Bay during the American Revolution, never had to worry about losing his job. It seems his wife was the mistress of General Henry Clinton, the general who commanded the British troops that occupied New York from 1776 to 1783.

Not everyone in Brooklyn was sympathetic to the abolition cause. During the Civil War, the *Brooklyn Eagle* was so outspoken in favor of slavery that at one point, the federal government revoked its mailing privileges.

Did you know that the playwright Arthur Miller had as many as six different residences in Brooklyn, most of which were in Brooklyn Heights?

After the Civil War, at 271 Ninth Street, Charles M. Higgins began the manufacture of Higgins India Ink, which is still the leading India ink brand today. Ironically, the product was misnamed—this black waterproof ink used in many professions from calligraphy to engineering really originated in China, not India.

Being the biggest investor in the New York Bridge Company—the organization that provided the initial financing of the Brooklyn Bridge—paid off handsomely for William Kingsley, a wealthy Brooklyn contractor. He profited not only by selling his stock when the cost of construction was taken over by governmental sources, but also by being given the job of chief contractor for the construction.

You can bet that two men who were leaders in their field will never be chosen to join their fellow Brooklynites in the Brooklyn Botanic Garden's Celebrity Walk even though they were born in Brooklyn and grew up here. One is Johnny Torrio, who became Chicago's number 1 crime boss in the 1920s and is credited with organizing the Mafia in different cities into a nationwide organization; the other is his protégé, Al Capone, who succeeded him in Chicago and became America's best-known gangster.

Anyone interested in the history of Brooklyn shouldn't miss going to the museum in the Brooklyn Navy Yard.

In the list of well-known journalists who once wrote for the original *Brooklyn Eagle*, there is one name that never seems to turn up—i.e., that of Alvah Bessie, one of the Hollywood Ten, who was a critic there early in his career.

Did you know that Mark Twain's *Innocents Abroad*, his best-selling book during his lifetime, was based on a trip made to Europe and the Holy Land in 1867 by members of Plymouth Church in Brooklyn Heights? Twain accompanied the group as a journalist.

George Tilyou, the owner of Coney Island's Steeplechase Park, never missed a trick. When the park burned down in 1906—then rebuilt the next year, it went on to the year 1964—he posted a sign the day after the fire announcing that, for a fee, visitors could view the ashes.

What do musical composers Ned Rorem, Paul Hindemith, John Adams, Ralph Vaughan Williams, Roger Sessions, and Leonard Bernstein have in common? They all composed music to poems of Brooklyn's Walt Whitman.

Pratt Institute is not the only educational institution that Thomas Pratt funded. He was also a financial supporter of Brooklyn's Adelphi Academy.

One of the most successful Brooklyn businessmen in the nineteenth century was Thomas Carman, a merchant who made a fortune in the 1850s when he went to Australia and sold small cooking stoves to the miners in that country's gold rush. While there, he also set up Australia's first stagecoach line.

Take your pick. One source says the subway station at Coney Island's Stillwell Avenue is the largest in the world. Another qualifies this by saying it is the largest in North America.

One of the largest crowds assembled in Brooklyn Heights—some several thousand people—was when Theodore Roosevelt came here in 1900 while campaigning for the governorship of New York State. According to the *NY Times*, which covered the event, he ate dinner that night in a restaurant on Montague Street.

I wonder how many people know that in the 1860s the Mexican General Santa Anna, who overwhelmed the Texans in the Battle of the Alamo, spent several years in exile in Staten Island.

Did you know that in 1896, New York had one of its worst heat waves? It was a heat wave many times worse than the one we are experiencing. Described as the "worst urban heat-related disaster in urban history," it saw temperatures in a nine-day period in August rise as high as 120 degrees—yes, 120 degrees—at a time there was no such thing as air-conditioning, refrigerators, or cooling centers. More than 1,300 New Yorkers died, and every day several hundred horses collapsed dead in the streets. The only bright spot—if there could be considered one—was that New York's police commissioner distributed free ice at one point. His name was Theodore Roosevelt.

According to some historians, it was Peter Stuyvesant who introduced tea to America. Supposedly, he brought it with him from Europe when he arrived in 1647 to take his post as director general of the Dutch West Indies colony of New Amsterdam.

If anyone asks you what song the victorious Dodgers sang to manager Walt Alston at the

Bossert Hotel when they were celebrating their victory in the 1955 World Series, you can tell them it was "For He's a Jolly Good Fellow."

If you think the New York subway system carries more passengers annually than any other subway in the world, you are mistaken. At least three other cities have subways that carry more—Tokyo, Moscow, and Seoul.

You could write a history of famous American bands by just noting the bands that played during the summers at Manhattan Beach through the years. In the late nineteenth century, there was John Philip Sousa and Pat Gilmore; in the 1920s, Paul Whiteman, Ben Bernie, and Ted Lewis; and in the 1930s to the 1940s, Artie Shaw, Benny Goodman, and Tommy Dorsey.

The Lenape Indians were the first Native American tribe to sign a treaty with the US government. Near the end of the American Revolution, an agreement was reached whereby they supplied scouts and warriors to the Continental Army in exchange for food and security.

In the early 1800s, when Brooklynites began talking about the possibility of building a bridge across the East River linking Brooklyn with

Manhattan, a man named Thomas Pope came forth with his idea, which was that of a flying pendant lever bridge, described as being "intensely original as well as impossible to build."

During World War II, a fully equipped artillery battery with anti-aircraft gun and barracks was installed at Sea Gate. It wasn't completely dismantled until the 1970s.

There was once a cable car that ran down Montague Street from Borough Hall to the East River. Described at the time as "the most successful cable car operation in the East," it was built in the 1890s to carry passengers to and from the Wall Street Ferry whose terminus was at the end of Montague Street. In 1904, the cable line was converted to an electric trolley line that continued running down Montague Street until 1924 even though the ferry had stopped running a decade before.

Years ago, when the Brooklyn Children's Museum was housed in two antique mansions in Brower Park, one of its most popular activities as far as the children were concerned was a weekend butterfly hunt.

Many visitors to Coney Island in the years before World War II didn't realize it, but the man who ran the sideshow exhibit featuring living premature babies was a licensed physician. His name was Dr. Martin Arthur Couney.

In Prohibition days, one of the most popular restaurants serving illegal beer and whiskey was the Red Hook Restaurant situated in Downtown Brooklyn next door to the Kings County Democratic Club.

So many Dutch people in New Amsterdam buried their family members on their own property that in 1660 and 1664, laws were enacted calling for all deceased to be buried in parish graveyards. Burials in public cemeteries like Green-Wood Cemetery came a century later.

When Jimmy Durante and Eddie Cantor were singing waiters at Coney Island before World War I, not only did they encourage Nathan Handwerker (Nathan's Famous) to leave Feltman's Restaurant, where he had been an employee, and start up his own hot dog stand, but they also gave him his start-up financing.

In the late nineteenth century, the Society of Old Brooklynites was able to obtain from the British War Office the names of eight thousand prisoners of war that were held in the British prison ships anchored in Wallabout Bay during the American Revolution.

When Coney Island's Parachute Jump was originally erected at the 1939 New York World's Fair—it was transferred to Steeplechase Park in 1941—it was called the Life Savers Corporation Parachute Tower because it was part of the Life Savers Exhibit.

It wasn't only the English and Hessian troops that fought the Continentals in the American Revolution. There were also the American Loyalists, one of the most prominent of whom was Oliver De Lancey, a member of the wealthy De Lancey family of lower Manhattan. Commissioned a major general in the British Army, he not only supplied valuable advice about Brooklyn to help Lord Howe crush George Washington in the Battle of Brooklyn, but he also took over the military command of Long Island during the British occupation. As if that wasn't enough, he supplied—and personally paid for—three battalions of New York Loyalists to join the British troops in their operations around the New York–New Jersey area.

The Bedford-Stuyvesant "neighborhood" is really composed of four neighborhoods: (1) Bedford,

(2) Stuyvesant Heights, (3) Ocean Hill, and (4) Weeksville.

Although there are pockets of what remains of the Lenape Indians in different parts of the United States, the main body is in Oklahoma, where these Native Americans relocated in the late nineteenth century.

In the 1830s, Arthur Benson, president of Brooklyn Gas, tried to develop the neighborhood we now call Bensonhurst as a better alternative to Coney Island for those who wanted to buy homes near the ocean. "Bensonhurst by the Sea," he advertised, "where some of the most refined, intelligent, and cultured New York and Brooklyn homeowners have bought their homes."

At one point, in Greenpoint it paid to be related to an early pioneer named Pieter Praa since a good part of the land was owned by one or another of his grandsons or sons-in-law.

It's interesting to note, in regard to those Admiral's Row houses in the old Brooklyn Navy Yard, that although the US government closed the yard in the 1960s, the houses continued to be occupied by navy personnel well into the 1970s.

Before Flatlands became Flatlands, its name was Nieuw Amersfoort, named for a town with a similar name in Holland. The change came when the British took over from the Dutch in 1664.

One of the more unusual functions of the ballroom of the old St. George Hotel was its use—because of its acoustics—as a recording studio. In 1957, Leonard Bernstein and the New York Philharmonic recorded Tchaikovsky's "Romeo and Juliet" there for Columbia Records.

The residents of Dyker Heights have picked an unusual adjective to describe their neighborhood. Its motto is "Dyker Heights is the Handsomest Suburb in Brooklyn."

He was born in England to American parents, and in 1859 he was a twenty-two-year-old chemist in Brooklyn who patented a petroleum jelly product that is still in almost every American's medicine cabinet today. The product was Vaseline. The inventor was Robert Chesebrough, who ended up not only very wealthy but also with a knighthood given him by Queen Victoria, who said at the time that she used Vaseline regularly for her skin. As for Robert Chesebrough, it is said that every day of his life until he died at 101 years, he ate a spoonful of the product he invented.

Did you know there are an estimated six thousand acres of park land in Brooklyn?

Boys High School in Brooklyn has many famous graduates, but one that is seldom mentioned— although he was once one of Hollywood's most powerful executives—is Irving Thalberg, the one-time head of production for MGM.

Among the military units from Brooklyn that participated in the Civil War, none was more colorful than the National Guard unit that had the nickname of "The Red-Legged Devils."

After he came to the United States in the early nineteenth century to embark on his bridge-building career, John Roebling learned that oil had been discovered on the property he had left behind in Saxonburg, Germany.

If not for a surveillance camera installed at the Gil Hodges Memorial Bridge to check automobile traffic, we wouldn't have a filmed record of the tragic airplane crash in 2001 of American Airlines Flight 587 over Belle Harbor, Queens, which took the lives of 260 passengers and 5 people on the ground.

If you want to know why the Coney Island Athletic Club no longer staged any heavyweight championship bouts after the famous 1899 fight between James J. Jeffries and sailor Tom Sharkey, it is because soon after—thanks to "do-gooders"—all professional boxing matches were banned in New York State for the next two decades.

The original *Brooklyn Daily Eagle* never gave up boosting Brooklyn even when derogatory remarks about the borough appeared in print. In Edmund Wilson's controversial novel *Memoirs of Hecate County*, which was banned in many US states, the author didn't have any nice things to say about Brooklyn, describing it variously as "pretty miserable" and "dreary." But that didn't stop the *Eagle* when covering it in an article using the headline "Banned Book Praises Brooklyn."

So many Jewish people moved into Williamsburg after the completion of the Williamsburg Bridge in 1903 that it took only a few years before the neighborhood was called what it is still referred to today—"The Jerusalem of America."

George Tilyou who built Steeplechase Park, one of Coney Island's three great amusement parks, started his career on the beach at Coney Island selling boxes of Coney Island sand for five cents. If you wanted a small bottle of "genuine Coney Island seawater," that would be five more cents.

In case you want to know how high the "cabins" on Coney Island's Wonder Wheel swing are, the answer is 135 feet.

Many of the celebrities buried in Green-Wood Cemetery have had biographies written about them, but as far as I know, only one "resident," Lola Montez, has been the subject of a major film—in this case, *Lola Montes*, the 1955 masterpiece by Max Ophuls. Her real name was Eliza Gilbert (the name on her tombstone). Actually Irish, she took the name of Lola Montez and, in the mid-nineteenth century, performed her famous Spider Dance in theaters all over Europe and America, counting as her friends such literary giants as Honore de Balzac; Alexandre Dumas, père; and George Eliot and her lovers Franz Liszt and King Ludwig of Bavaria, who lost his throne because of his relationship with her. Ending up in New York, ailing and penniless, she died in 1861 still in her forties and got to Green-Wood thanks to an unknown female admirer who buried her in part of the admirer's family plot.

By rights, Bergen Street should really be Hansen Street. The man who came from Norway to set up his farm in Bergen Hill was Hans Hansen, but once he was here, he changed his name to Hans Bergen in honor of the town he came from.

It wasn't just because the cost of the subway to get to Coney Island in the early 1900s was only five cents that Coney Island got the nickname of "The Nickel Empire." It was also because, at one time, everything there cost only five cents, from a hot dog to a ride on a roller coaster.

The popular ailanthus tree—immortalized by Betty Smith in her novel *A Tree Grows in Brooklyn*—is not native to Brooklyn. It was brought to Brooklyn in the 1840s by entrepreneurs who were trying to establish a silk industry here and imported the tree, figuring its leaves would be a good food for silkworms. P.S. the worms didn't go for them; and as for the silk project, it never got off the ground.

Although Brooklyn bank robber Willie Sutton was famous for saying he robbed banks "because that's where the money is," he claimed he never said such a thing, and he attributed the quote to the author Quentin Reynolds, who wrote his biography.

You would never know when you look at the Brooklyn waterfront today that in the 1930s, it accounted for 55 percent of all the shipping commerce in the New York area.

Many people thought Abe "Kid Twist" Reles, the Murder Inc. killer, got his nickname from the way he killed his victims (putting an ice pick in their ears and twisting it); but actually, the name came from an earlier "Kid Twist" who was a one-time famous Manhattan gangster.

The baseball team that became the Brooklyn Dodgers wasn't exactly a world-beater when it joined the National League. From 1891 to 1897, it finished out of the second division only once and didn't hit pay dirt until 1898 when Ned Hanlon, the manager of the Baltimore Orioles, purchased half ownership of the Brooklyn team and moved his Oriole stars—like Willie Keeler and Hughie Jennings—into its lineup. The first year they arrived in Brooklyn, they walked away with the pennant.

Founded in 1854, Polytechnic Institute (now Polytechnic Institute of New York University) is the second oldest institution of its type in the United States.

Did you know that in 1917, two of America's top movie comedians, Fatty Arbuckle and Buster Keaton, made a movie in Coney Island titled— what else—*Coney Island*?

Although Lord Cornwallis ended up in Virginia when he surrendered the British Army at Yorktown to end the fighting in the Revolutionary War, he wasn't a stranger to Brooklyn. In the very first battle of the war, which took place in Brooklyn in August 1776, he was second-in-command of the British invasion forces, and at one point he made his headquarters in the Old Stone House.

The original planning for Prospect Park called for it to be closed at night. It wasn't that possible crime was an issue; rather, it was thought the scenic values of the park could not be fully appreciated in the dark.

Bensonhurst today is a far cry from what it was before the 1890s when it consisted of little more than the Benson farm.

The first electricity generator in Brooklyn is thought to have been the one that the BRT (later BMT) subway system installed in 1905.

It was the *Brooklyn Eagle* that sponsored broadcasting's first quiz show. Called the *Brooklyn Eagle Quiz on Current Events*, it was hosted by H. V. Kaltenborn, an *Eagle* editor who went on to fame as radio's first prominent newscaster. The date was 1925.

Although none of the seventeen leading newspapers in New York and Brooklyn sympathized with the

Southern States, only five supported Abraham Lincoln's policies in regard to state rights and slavery.

According to the *AIA Guide to New York City*, there is a small museum located in the Soldiers and Sailors Memorial Arch in Grand Army Plaza.

Why is it that so many people keep calling the Brooklyn Botanic Garden the Brooklyn "Botanical" Garden?

Although the central branch of the Brooklyn Public Library on Eastern Parkway opened its doors in 1941, it took another decade before the interior construction was completed.

Are the hundred-some members of the Knickerbocker Field Club in Flatbush aware that their club is the oldest tennis club in Brooklyn and that the five courts they play on are the same courts that were first played on in 1892?

Promotion in the US Army came very slowly in the years before the Civil War. In the 1840s, when Robert E. Lee was put in charge of improving the fortifications at Fort Hamilton and the other US forts in the Narrows, his rank was only that of a captain.

Domine Henricus Selyns, Brooklyn's first man of the cloth, didn't think too much of Brooklyn. He described it as "an ugly little village."

An early edition of the *AIA Guide to New York City* singled out the houses at 2 and 3 Pierrepont Place in Brooklyn Heights as the "most elegant brownstones in New York City."

In the late nineteenth century, there were half a dozen country clubs within the city limits. One that survived is the Knickerbocker Field Club in Flatbush at the corner of East Eighteenth Street and Tennis Court. Once featuring all sports from baseball to track, it still has its five original tennis courts that were first played on and is undoubtedly the oldest tennis club and outdoor tennis facility in Brooklyn, if not New York. Alas, its baseball diamond and track and its toboggan slide are gone. Also, the victim of vandals is its one-time elegant Victorian clubhouse with a bowling alley, library, and billiard room.

Did you know that when Brooklyn College started up in the 1920s in Downtown Brooklyn, it was known as "The Poor Man's College"?

According to the *AIA Guide to New York City*, the five-story house at 18 Sidney Place in Brooklyn

Heights is the tallest residential Greek Revival building in Brooklyn.

The factory building still stands at the back of the house at 168 Eighth Street in Park Slope where Charles M. Higgins in the nineteenth century developed his famous India ink product, which is still the leading product in its field today.

There was a two-day period in 1890 when the police in Brooklyn were faced with two stories of ghosts frightening inhabitants at night. The first sighting took place in Bushwick when a woman dressed in scanty attire with her hair disheveled was seen running in bare feet and becoming hysterical when approached. The second took place the following night when another ghost was supposedly seen near the Brooklyn-Queens border. In both cases, several hundred police were dispatched to search the areas, but from the time they returned saying they had seen nothing, no more ghosts were reported.

In 1851, after the New York State Legislature passed legislation permitting the establishment of public cemeteries, a group of Brooklynites organized the Citizens Union Cemetery for persons of color who died poor. There was no charge for the burials. The only cost was for opening and closing the ground.

Although the statues of Henry Ward Beecher in Columbus Park and Plymouth Church of the Pilgrims look somewhat the same, they had different sculptors. The one in Columbus Park was sculpted by John Quincy Adams Ward, the one in Plymouth Church by Gutzon Borglum of Mount Rushmore fame.

Although the overall name for the Native Americans who inhabited Brooklyn before the Dutch came was *Lenape*, those who lived in the individual Indian villages called themselves by the areas they lived in. Thus, those who lived in Nayack called themselves Nayacks, while those who lived in Canarsie called themselves Canarsies.

One reason that some think there still might be one or two nineteenth-century railroad locomotives buried in the part of the underground tunnel under Atlantic Avenue that hasn't been explored yet is that in the lists of locomotives kept by the Long Island Railroad, there are two engines from the mid-1800s that were never marked off as having been decommissioned.

Did you know that Brooklyn once had a movie theater that specialized in showing foreign films? It was the Momarte, a small five-hundred-seat theater next to the RKO Orpheum on Fulton Street. It opened in 1927 and lasted until 1956.

When it comes to baseball history, the nineteenth-century Brooklyn Excelsiors deserve a special place because two pitchers on this team invented standard pitches still used in professional baseball today—the curveball (first pitched by Charles Cummings) and the fastball (first pitched by James Creighton).

Although one of the star attractions of the recently instituted Brooklyn Navy Yard tours is Quarters A, the former Commandant's House and a National Landmark possibly designed by Charles Bulfinch (one of the architects of the US Capitol)—through some governmental quirk, the building has been in private hands since 1971.

Believe it or not, you can still purchase Ariosa, the first national coffee brand, which was originally produced by Brooklyn's Arbuckle Coffee Co. in the 1860s and has now been revived by a company in Arizona. Known as "The Coffee That Won the West," Ariosa—because of its special formula, which enabled it to be used in a skillet without the coffee becoming discolored—was an important factor in the life of the frontier, an essential in the chuck wagons of all the cowboys riding the western ranges from Montana to New Mexico. It was so popular that, as one source said, "in the West in the nineteenth century, no one knew there was any other brand of coffee."

When the British took over from the Dutch West India Co. in 1664, they changed as many Dutch place-names as they could to English names— New York for New Amsterdam, Brookland for Breuckelen, and even the destination of the Brooklyn Ferry across the East River, which they called Dover as a reminder of their English background.

The rest of the world called them paddy wagons, but to Brooklyn's police force in the nineteenth century, they were "hoodlum wagons."

Do those who live in Cobble Hill know that there was once a street in Williamsburg named Smith Street that, before the annexation of Williamsburg by Brooklyn, was renamed Humboldt Street in honor of the German scientist Alexander von Humboldt?

The population of Kings County grew so rapidly from 1923 to 1927 that it led all the other counties in the United States in housing starts.

Do the patients in the Cobble Hill Health Center at 380 Henry Street know that its building was originally St. Peters Hospital, part of a large complex that also included a school (St. Peters Academy), a home for working girls, and a church (St. Peters)?

Green-Wood Cemetery is not the only cemetery in Brooklyn with notables among its interred. Among those buried there are W. R. Grace (businessman), Gil Hodges (baseball star), Diamond Jim Brady (Gay Nineties bon vivant), Sunny Jim Fitzsimmons (racehorse trainer), Willie Sutton (bank robber), and Frankie Yale (gangster).

Hezekiah Pierrepont's Anchor Gin distillery, located at the end of Joralemon Street in Brooklyn Heights, was the first gin distillery in the United States.

Yes, it's true. Until it was torn down in 1903 after being unoccupied for years, Brooklyn had a haunted house. Called Melrose Hall, it was located on Bedford Avenue between Winthrop Street and Clarkson Avenue. According to locals who explored it, it had all the trappings of scary movie, including sliding wall panels, mysterious passageways, and subterranean tunnels.

Here is a follow-up on additional locations in Brooklyn of some of those late nineteenth-century police precinct stations that resembled Moorish palaces and medieval castles: 4th Precinct at the corner of Classon and Dekalb Avenues, 13th Precinct on Congress Street between Amity and Emmett Streets, 17th Precinct corner Liberty and Miller Avenues, and 18th Precinct Fourth Avenue and Forty-Third Street.

Question: What do the following mayors of Greater New York have in common besides the fact their terms of office were in the twentieth century—i.e., Abraham Beame, Joseph V. McKee, Ardolf [sic] Kline, and George McClellan Jr.? Answer: Not a highway, street, bridge, school, park, or housing development has been named for them.

When Brooklyn's first municipal laws were issued in 1822, they contained a provision that the town's bread should be made of "wholesome flour" and be weighed accurately. Any baker who failed to comply would be fined forty pence.

Geraldine Ferraro was not the only New York woman who blazed political trails for women. So did Brooklyn-born Elizabeth Holtzman. Not only did she make a name for herself as a congresswoman, but before that she also had been the first (and only) woman to be district attorney of Kings County and the first (and only) woman who served as New York City Controller.

In its special expanded newspaper edition for December 31, 1899, the *Brooklyn Eagle* made all sorts of predictions—ranging from garbage being transported away in trucks to electricity replacing steam as the major power source—as to what Brooklyn could expect in the forthcoming twentieth century. Although its predictions were considered outlandish at the time, critics later had to admit that most had come true, and in commenting on this, one wag pointed out, however, that the one prediction the *Eagle* missed out on completely was the story of its own demise as a newspaper in 1955.

Did you know that at one point Washington A. Roebling, the engineer in charge of constructing the Brooklyn Bridge, was so depressed about his physical condition—he had gotten the bends in supervising the building of the caissons—he considered resigning his job and actually wrote a letter to that effect. Whether the letter was ever sent or, if sent, was ignored is not known, but whatever the case, he never did resign.

Not until 1898 did the Brooklyn, Flatbush, and Jamaica Plank Road Company close down its toll gates and stop charging tolls for vehicles that passed over its roadway.

Talk about coincidences. Only three weeks ago in this *Aerie* column, I noted that in 1898 a detachment of nurses from Long Island College Hospital took special leave to help out in the medical treatment of the wounded in the Spanish-American War. Now with MDs and nurses so badly needed in the Gulf area in the aftermath of Katrina, the Continuum Health Partners—of which LICH is a member, along with Beth Israel and St. Luke's Roosevelt—is sending a contingent of one hundred staff members to help out.

When the first municipal baths were established in Brooklyn in the nineteenth century, they were open every day except Sunday. Four days a week they were for men, two days for women.

Not only did Bill Clinton stop off at Junior's when he was on the campaign trail, but so did John F. Kennedy when he came to Brooklyn seeking votes. What he ordered was strawberry shortcake.

Diamond Jim Brady lived up to his name when he visited Coney Island in the Gay Nineties. When he ventured down the Boardwalk, he had on his feet diamond-studded sandals.

Unlike many of Brooklyn's neighborhoods where the prominent residents were of Dutch descent, in Brooklyn Heights the dominant families— like the Pierreponts—were New Englanders. The grandfather of Hezekiah Pierrepont was the original minister of the New Haven colony.

According to linguists, the so-called Brooklyn accent is dying out.

You would expect William S. Hart, Hollywood's first Western superstar, to be buried in California. After all, there is a Williams A. Hart School and a William S. Hart Park in Los Angeles. But his grave is actually three thousand miles away in Brooklyn's Green-Wood Cemetery.

William Kingsley was not only the owner of the *Brooklyn Eagle* once but also a contractor—indeed through his connections, the chief contractor—in the building of the Brooklyn Bridge. Although the facts are murky, he supposedly had a deal whereby he got a royalty amounting to 25 percent of every dollar expended on the bridge's construction.

Did you know it was not until the late 1860s that the merry-go-rounds at Coney Island were converted to run on steam power?

It was not an easy time for the citizens of Brooklyn when the British Army occupied the city during the

Revolutionary War. Elections were forbidden, civil courts were suspended, prices were fixed on many foods, and some two thousand Brooklyn men were impressed into service to help build a British fort in Brooklyn Heights.

When Walt Whitman was editor of the *Brooklyn Eagle*, he called it as it was in the obituaries he wrote. In the case of the death of one Samuel Leggett, he wrote, "This man is dead. He was at one time . . . president of the Franklin Bank just previous to its failure, under the most abominable circumstances, he acquired a splendid property, and was at the time of his death a large owner of real estate . . . He had some good qualities."

It's not true, as some believe, that Leif Eriksson Park in Bay Ridge was at one time supposed to have been named for Mother Cabrini.

According to screen star Susan Hayward—who was born in Brooklyn and who won the Academy Award in 1955 for her role in *I Want to Live*— she never would have made out in Hollywood if a studio speech expert had not worked with her to lose her Brooklyn accent.

Did you know that among the several neighborhoods in Brooklyn where the great

Italian tenor Enrico Caruso sang during World War I to promote the sale of US war bonds was Sheepshead Bay?

Because the food inspection laws were so lax a century ago, at one point when Nathan's Famous started up in the early 1900s, it dressed all those serving up its hot dogs in white surgical gowns—like what physicians wear—to suggest its products were safe to eat.

What started hundreds of pedestrians panicking on the Brooklyn Bridge a week after its opening in 1883 was that a woman coming down the stairs on the Brooklyn side lost her footing and fell to the ground. Mistakenly assuming the bridge was about to collapse, everyone rushed to get off, with the result that twelve people died in the crush.

In 1816 when Brooklyn was incorporated as a village, it was a mile square in size stretching from what is now the end of Old Fulton Street to Borough Hall, and its population was four thousand.

Almost everyone knows that when the Dodgers decided to take on a black baseball player in 1947, they chose Jackie Robinson; but how many know that the second black player taken on by the Dodgers soon afterward was Roy Campanella?

In case you forgot, Jimmy Breslin's classic book *The Gang That Couldn't Shoot Straight* was about Joey Gallo and his fellow gangsters in Red Hook.

Did you know that the new state-of-the-art industrial building that just opened in the Brooklyn Navy Yard is the first LEED-certified multistory building constructed in the United States?

The only church in New York City ever attended by Abraham Lincoln was Henry Ward Beecher's Plymouth Church in Brooklyn Heights. He worshipped there twice—a week apart—in 1859 when he came to New York to make his famous speech at Manhattan's Cooper Union, which resulted in him becoming the Republican candidate for the presidency and, ultimately, the president.

John V. McKane was "boss" of Coney Island in the late nineteenth century. He controlled everything from renting bathing suits to selling waterfront properties. He never stopped telling everyone that he was responsible for electing Benjamin Harrison as the president of the United States in 1886. It seems that in this close election in which Harrison lost the popular vote but gained the electoral vote,

New York was a crucial swing state, and what possibly turned the tide for Harrison was the fact that in Coney Island—which had 1,500 registered voters—Harrison received six thousand votes, thanks to McKane's addition of names from Green-Wood and Washington cemeteries. True or not, when McKane and a hundred of his fellow Coney Islanders marched in Harrison's inaugural parade in Washington, DC, the new president was seen acknowledging his presence by waving to him.

Are those living in the apartments in the Ansonia Court complex at Twelfth Street between Seventh and Eighth Avenues aware that when their building was the factory of the Ansonia Clock Co., the biggest watch company in the world, as many as 1,500 employees worked there?

Although the Erie Canal ostensibly ended at Albany, its actual terminus was at either the Atlantic or Erie Basins in Red Hook because that is where all the grain that came from the Midwest was stored, which had been shipped first to Buffalo via Lake Erie, then barged down the Erie Canal to Albany, and finally sent down the Hudson River to Basins' warehouses to be stored for further distribution.

Not all the trolleys in the early 1900s were used for transportation alone. There was one car named Columbia—more ornate than the usual trolley—which was operated by the Brooklyn Heights Railroad for use in excursions where a buffet lunch complete with tables and silverware would be offered as the trolley car traveled around the borough.

In the early twentieth century, there was a brewery in Brooklyn named the Consumers Park Brewery, which was the first electric brewery in the United States. Its generators generated so much electricity that the brewery was able to supply free electricity to many of the homes in the neighborhood.

For much of his life, the playwright Arthur Miller lived in Brooklyn Heights on no less than five different streets—Pierrepont, Schermerhorn, Montague, Grace Court, and Columbia Heights.

In researching the former Ex-Lax building on Atlantic Avenue, one of the first factory buildings in Brooklyn to be converted into residences, I found out where the name of the company and brand came from. Namely, from Excellent Laxative.

As a mayor of New York City in the early 1900s, William J. Gaynor left his mark in several ways. One, unlike all other mayors, he had once studied for the priesthood. Two, he got a law passed allowing baseball to be played on Sundays in public parks, saying that this "was better for boys than temptations I need not mention." Three, he walked to his office in New York's City Hall from his residence in Park Slope. Four, he was the only New York City mayor to be the victim of an (unsuccessful) assassination attempt when a discharged city worker shot him in the throat as he and his wife were boarding an ocean liner en route to a European vacation.

This is how Walt Whitman described the almost two dozen breweries that once thrived in Bushwick in the nineteenth century: "They are the source of the mighty outpourings of ale and lager beer, refreshing the thirsty lovers of those liquids in hot and cold weather."

The information published in the *Jerusalem Post* several years ago, which said Winston Churchill was part Jewish because his father-in-law, Brooklyn's Leonard Jerome, was a member of the Jewish faith, is considered absurd. However, not unbelievable—and several times even repeated by Winston himself—is the current thinking among historians that his mother, Jennie Jerome, had Iroquois blood in her.

There couldn't have been a more dismal ending on September 24, 1957, the last day the Dodgers played at Ebbets Field, than when the last batter, Gil Hodges, went to bat and struck out.

In 1914 when Brooklyn's Vitagraph Film Studio released its movie epic *Battle Cry of Peace*, it advertised it as being the story of Hiram Maxim, the inventor of the machine gun, and said it had a peace-loving theme. But leading pacifists condemned it as being militaristic, and Henry Ford claimed it was propaganda financed by the munitions industry.

Of all the well-known writers associated with Brooklyn, none was more prolific than Irwin Shaw who once lived in Bushwick and was a graduate of Brooklyn College. He wrote not only plays like "Bury the Dead," best-selling novels like *The Young Lions*, scenarios for hit movies like *Commandos Strike at Dawn*, and award-winning short stories like "Girls in Their Summer Dresses" and "Sailor from the Bremen," but also several long-running television series.

Did you know that although Governors Island is only a stone's throw away from Brooklyn—just across Buttermilk Channel—it is legally part of Manhattan, which is a half mile away?

The dining room at Pete's Downtown Restaurant at the corner of Water Street and Old Fulton Street is all that remained of a once-famous nineteenth-century Brooklyn hotel—the Franklin House.

The British army that routed George Washington's Continental troops in the Battle of Brooklyn was commanded by two brothers—Sir William Howe, who was in charge of the land forces, and Lord Richard Howe, who headed up the naval forces.

Although LeMarcus Thompson was called the Father of Gravity Rides (he built the nation's first gravity-powered roller coaster and also the popular gravity switch-back scenic railroad at Coney Island), his inventions didn't stop with amusement park attractions. He is also given credit for inventing seamless women's hosiery.

When George Jessel made a personal appearance at the Brooklyn Paramount in the 1930s, the theater and streets around it became so crowded that Mayor LaGuardia rushed over from New York City fearing there was a possibility of a riot.

Although the Educational Alliance is strongly identified with Manhattan's Lower East Side, when it started up in 1889 it was located in Brooklyn in Williamsburg.

Brooklyn Heights' landmark St. George Hotel not only had more rooms than any other hotel in New York at one time—2,632 by count—but also the greatest number of windows—over 6,000.

If not for a group of members of Brooklyn's Plymouth Church who sent Abraham Lincoln $200 to come to New York to speak, he might never have become president, for it was the speech he gave at New York's Cooper Union on that visit that drew national attention and made him the Republican candidate for the presidency. (PS. A copy of the telegram offering him the $200 is in the archives of Plymouth Church of the Pilgrims.)

When you think of Walt Whitman, you automatically think of Brooklyn. However, he was not born in Brooklyn (he was born on Long Island), he didn't die in Brooklyn (he died in Camden, New Jersey), and the last thirty years of his life he spent away from Brooklyn (in Camden and Washington, DC).

One of the big moments at Floyd Bennett Field was in 1932 when twenty-four seaplanes from Italy under the command of General Italo Balbo landed on their way to the Chicago World's Fair.

Whatever the final US Census number is for the population of Brooklyn this year, I doubt it will come close to the population of our borough in 1950 before so many Brooklynites moved out to suburbs in New Jersey and Long Island: 2,738,175.

One of the most famous (and notorious) persons buried in Green-Wood Cemetery was Emma Cunningham, accused of the stabbing of her lover, Dr. Harvey Burdell, a wealthy Manhattan dentist. At her trial she produced a certificate claiming she had married Burdell and said she was carrying his child (although she refused to allow a doctor to examine her). Acquitted, she was stalked by the prosecutor who, convinced of her guilt, discovered she had tried to adopt a baby. Exposed, she admitted the marriage certificate was a fake, and she relinquished her rights to Burdell's $80,000 estate. In 2007, a new stone was placed over her grave, which is not far from Burdell's. On it are the words "May God Rest Her Troubled Soul."

Did you know it was the wife of Nathan Handwerker, the founder of Nathan's Famous, who developed the recipe used in the company's hot dogs?

During the 1950s, when large segments of the Brooklyn population moved away to Long Island or New Jersey, one of the few neighborhoods to gain in population was Sheepshead Bay. The reason is that there was a large influx of Jews from Crown Heights, Williamsburg, and Bushwick.

Seven years before the construction of the Brooklyn Bridge was completed in 1883, those cellars under the bridge on the Manhattan side were being used for storage of wines and other products.

In the days when the Dutch and New Netherland controlled the area, the seat of government for Long Island, which included the six towns of what is now Brooklyn, was in the town of Flatbush.

Although the term *Dodgers* when applied to the Brooklyn Dodgers conjures up scenes of playful antics as pedestrians tried to dodge the oncoming trolleys, it was actually far more serious. In the one year alone of 1894, along just one trolley route from Flatbush to East New York, there were eighteen people killed in trolley accidents.

In the nineteenth century when William "Boss" Tweed died, everyone wondered how it was possible he was able to be buried in Brooklyn's Green-Wood Cemetery when the cemetery had a rule that no one released from prison could ever be interred there. But the family pressed the issue, claiming that Green-Wood should make an exception since

Tweed had already purchased a lot there years before. A compromise was finally reached, with the cemetery relenting on the condition that the family accepted to make the gravestone a "modest" one.

The number that Dodger great Duke Snider wore on his uniform, number 4, was his favorite number because it was also the number of his favorite player, who was not a Dodger but a Yankee—Lou Gehrig.

Did you know the greenhouse at McGovern-Weir Florists at Fifth Avenue and Twenty-Fifth Street across Green-Wood Cemetery came from the 1904 St. Louis World's Fair? It was shipped here after the fair was over.

There were two Pierrepont mansions in Brooklyn Heights. One called Four Chimneys stood on what is now Montague Street, approximately where the Heights Casino is. The other was at the end of Pierrepont Street, where the playground is now.

Those Coney Island yards where the railroad cars are kept is the largest subway maintenance facility in the world.

During the American Revolution, no Loyalist made a bigger effort to help the British than Oliver De Lancey, a member of the De Lancey family, which had large holdings in Manhattan's Lower East Side. On his own and with his own money, De Lancey formed a brigade of 1,500 New Yorkers to fight with the British; and during the English occupation, as a brigadier general in the British Army, he was put in control of all the English troops on Long Island, which included the six towns that eventually made up Brooklyn.

Technically, it's not completely true that Brooklyn never won a national baseball pennant until 1955. In the late nineteenth century when Brooklyn had several major teams, the Brooklyn Atlantics became the number 1 team in all US baseball when it won a game against the seemingly invincible Cincinnati Red Stockings who had played seventy-eight games in two years without one loss.

Brooklyn Bridge Park makes its film debut in *Carnage*, the new motion picture starring Jodie Foster and Kate Winslet. Indeed, besides Brooklyn Bridge Park, there is only one other setting in the entire film—the interior of an apartment in what is presumably a luxury condo in DUMBO.

More on Tom Johnson, the nineteenth-century trolley magnate. Although he controlled trolley lines in half a dozen US cities and lived in Brooklyn only briefly, he is buried in Brooklyn's Green-Wood Cemetery.

When the conversion of the former Domino Sugar Building in Willamsburg is completed, those who will have apartments there will be able to say that at the turn of the last century their building was the leading factory of the so-called Sugar Trust, which produced 90 percent—yes, 90 percent—of the nation's refined sugar.

We can thank Mrs. Edward C. Blum, wife of the one-time president of the Abraham & Straus department store (now Macy's), for making the forsythia Brooklyn's official flower. It was she who persuaded the Brooklyn Borough president to make the designation legal in 1940.

Nathan's Famous says that one reason its hot dogs always seem to taste better when purchased at its original Coney Island stand at Surf and Stillwell Avenues is because Coney Island's salt water makes the difference.

Because of the large number of Norwegians in Bay Ridge, Bay High School (now the High School for Telecommunications) once included courses in Norwegian in its curriculum.

Did you know that the architect for the Federal Building on Tillary Street in Downtown Brooklyn, Cesar Pelli, also designed the two Petronas Towers in Kuala Lumpur, which were the tallest buildings in the world from 1998 to 2004?

Although Brooklyn Heights is one of the most elite neighborhoods in Brooklyn today, it wasn't always that way. In the 1930s and 1940s, many of its brownstones turned into rooming houses, and some sections—particularly those where the Mitchell-Lama apartments were built—were considered slums.

Coney Island's Dreamland, the 1900s amusement park, deserves credit for being one of the first commercially air-conditioned enterprises in the United States. It was installed in the amusement park's Swiss Village in order to chill the atmosphere to produce extra chilling climate to approximate that of the original Swiss Alps.

During World War, the membership of the swank Crescent Athletic Club on Pierrepont Street opened its rifle range to nonmembers who wanted to sharpen their marksmanship. The gesture was made, as one member expressed, to improve "military awareness."

I wonder how many of those who live at the Cadman Plaza apartment complex at 75 Henry Street refer to it by its official name of Whitman Close?

According to one account, the first prostitute in New Netherland in colonial days was one Griet Reynierrs, a former barmaid in Amsterdam.

The first great fire in Brooklyn was in 1849. More than two hundred homes were destroyed, along with three churches and the post office.

When Walt Whitman was an editor of the *Brooklyn Eagle*, he attacked those who were trying to urbanize the area around Fort Greene Park. He said it would be the same as if in Manhattan building lots were sold in Washington Square, blind alleys run in Tomkins Park, and the Battery was erased.

It was an oil refiner named Abraham Geissner in Williamsburg who, in connection with marketing his lamp oil, coined the word *kerosene*.

Did you know that in the early days in Brooklyn history, not only was tobacco grown, but also cotton?

As an example of how deadly the Civil War was to those who fought in it, of the 1,000 soldiers of a

Brooklyn Army regiment called the Phalanx who marched off to fight the Confederacy, only 232 returned.

The original name of the Jehovah's Witnesses was the Watch Tower Bible and Tract Society. The name change took place in 1931, when J. F. Rutherford became president.

In a ceremony held at a Cyclones game several years ago, when pitcher Danny Devitt and catcher Joe Pignatano repeated the respective roles they played in the last Brooklyn Dodger game in Ebbetts Field in 1955, the crowd in the ballpark was larger than it had been in the actual last game played in 1955.

Did you know that the Brooklyn Battery Tunnel runs under Governors Island?

It was the Brooklyn Paramount that introduced jazz to Brooklyn when, in the early 1930s, it featured such artists as Duke Ellington, Dizzy Gillespie, and Miles Davis.

The response of the Brooklyn Heights community to do something about the helicopters overhead reminds me of other mass movements in the neighborhood (all successful) to thwart encroachment, such as the 1950s opposition to

Robert Moses's plan to run the BQE through its streets and a century-ago protest to put a subway stop in the St. George Hotel when the initial plans called for trains to run from Manhattan to Brooklyn without any access from the Heights.

In the 1930s, there were two Fannie Farmer candy stores in Brooklyn Heights—one on Henry Street and the other on Court Street.

When a list is made of famous aviators who once flew out of Floyd Bennett Field, the name of Charles Lindbergh is often included, along with Howard Hughes, Amelia Earhart, Wiley Post, and Douglas "One-Way" Corrigan. Alas, Lindbergh's epic solo flight across the Atlantic took place in 1927, five years before Floyd Bennett Field opened. The field Lindbergh flew from was Roosevelt Field in Long Island.

The last year any extensive farming was done in Brooklyn was 1925.

Do the residents of 117 Columbia Heights know their building was the Norwegian Club in the 1930s?

The Marine Roof was not the only famous dining spot in the Bossert Hotel in its heyday. There was also the Grill Room, which was designed by Joseph Urban, who was the architect for the Ziegfeld Theater in Manhattan and the Mar-A-Lago resort in Palm Beach, Florida.

Say what you want about immigrants, but in the case of the Brooklyn Bridge—Brooklyn's most famous landmark—it was an immigrant who designed it, and it was immigrants who built it.

Some typefaces never die. In doing research recently in old Brooklyn telephone directories, I found that the typeface used for names and addresses today seem to be the same as the one used in the directories of the 1950s.

More on Dr. Harvey Burdell, whose murder in 1857 was "the crime of the century" and who is buried in Green-Wood Cemetery, not far from his accused murderer, Emma Cunningham. He was hardly an upstanding gentleman. Described by his contemporaries as a sexual predator, real-estate swindler, and gambler who didn't pay his debts, on the eve of one of his marriages, he supposedly tried to extort money from his prospective father-in-law, who, as a result, cancelled the wedding.

You can't tell by looking at it, but the Hotel Bossert in Brooklyn Heights was built in two sections.

The front section facing Montague Street was built in 1908, while the second section facing Remsen Street was built five years later.

Although as many as five thousand women were employed at the Brooklyn Navy Yard during World War II, there wasn't one female working there twelve months after the war was over.

Did you know that there is a Hollywood legend entombed in Green-Wood Cemetery? He is the 1920s cowboy star William S. Hart. Not only is Hart's grave there, so are the graves of his family.

In 1784, when the original St. Ann's—Brooklyn's first Episcopal church—was founded on Sands Street, its church services were described as having "all the prestige that belonged to a parish of Trinity Church in Manhattan."

Long Island College Hospital—which is celebrating its 150th anniversary this year—ranks as the third major hospital to be established in Brooklyn, the first two being Kings County Medical Center (1833) and Brooklyn Hospital (1845).

In the 1920s, some of the nation's biggest and most expensive yachts tied up at the Tebo Boat Basin in Red Hook, among them J. P. Morgan's *Corsair*.

In case anyone asks you to name the four composers honored with a monument in Prospect Park's Music Grove, you can answer—Von Weber, Beethoven, Mozart, and Grieg.

Yes, there was a Mansion House Hotel on Hicks Street where the Mansion House apartments are now. It was torn down in the 1930s to make room for the present apartment complex.

The company that supplied electricity to Brooklyn before Con Edison took over had the name (not unsurprisingly) the Brooklyn Edison Company.

Did you know that the one-way traffic regulations on Pierrepont Street in Brooklyn Heights once called for automobiles and trucks to go from north to south instead of south to north as they do now?

The Commission that authorized the construction of the Brooklyn Bridge made just one change in the detailed plans drawn up by John Roebling, the bridge's original chef engineer. They changed the height of the central span from 130 feet to 135 feet.

In the 1920s, there was a move by real-estate developers to make Crown Heights one of Brooklyn's prime areas by replacing its Victorian brownstones with apartment houses that had elevators, half-timbered facades, and Tudor-sounding names. One such apartment house called Buckingham Hill Apartments advertised its location on St. Marks Avenue as "beyond comparison . . . on the most exclusive avenue in Brooklyn."

Did you know that until the 1930s when Mayor LaGuardia decided that pushcarts in the outdoor markets were unsanitary and that only indoor markets were acceptable, there were fifty-eight outdoor markets in the city and an estimated fourteen thousand pushcart peddlers?

During World War II, the site in Red Hook where IKEA is now building a retail outlet was where Todd Shipyards built the landing craft that took the troops across the English Channel to Normandy Beach on D-Day.

In Brooklyn, during Prohibition one of the better known establishments to flaunt the law was Oetjens, a famous seafood restaurant at 2210 Church Avenue. In the year of 1930 alone, it was raided by federal agents no less than three times.

The New York Police Department never had such a fallout as when Harry Gross—Brooklyn's number 1 bookmaker whose illegal operation grossed $20 million a year—turned state's evidence. Implicated in giving him "protection" were a police commissioner, a chief inspector, three deputy inspectors, four inspectors, three captains, and dozens of regular police officers. Gross said during his trial, "I paid off everyone. Everyone!"

In the 1930s, New York City's Board of Transportation ran ads in the local newspapers asking the public to support a pending bond issue that, if passed, would enable it to extend the Nostrand Avenue subway line to Sheepshead Bay and the Utica Avenue line to Flatlands. The bond issue passed, but as we know, the extensions were never made.

Not all who graduated from the prestigious Erasmus Hall High School in Flatbush had fond memories of their alma mater. According to Matthew Josephson, the author who became famous for coining the phrase *robber barons* in his best-selling book with that title, "It's a fancy grind factory."

Yes, the Blythebourne Post Office at New Utrecht and Fifty-First Street is where the Boro Park Theater used to be.

What brought down the linchpin of FDR's New Deal program—the Works Progress Administration (WPA)—were two Brooklyn brothers named Schechter who ran a small kosher butcher shop at 858 East Fifty-Second Street. To those who felt FDR went too far in the New Deal, they were national heroes when they took their case to the US Supreme Court, claiming the WPA was unfair to their business. But when the Court ruled in their favor saying the WPA was unconstitutional, they found it a Pyrrhic victory since their legal fees totaled $22,000—a sum that virtually bankrupted them.

I don't know whether it will be brought out in the new HBO series on John Adams, but it was he who, when president, was responsible for taking a small shipyard on Wallabout Bay and developing it into what became the Brooklyn Navy Yard.

Several years ago, the *Wall Street Journal* broke the story that Bobby Thomson's historic home run was the result of the Giants stealing the signals of the Brooklyn team. Now the source of that story, author Joshua Prager, has added more details in a book titled *The Echoing Green: The Untold Story of Bobby Thomson, Ralph Branca and the Shot Heard Round the World*. It says that the theft was carried out via a telescope hidden behind a mesh grid of a clubhouse window in the Polo Grounds.

One of the many reasons that Deno's Wonder Wheel at Coney Island should be proud on its one hundredth anniversary this year is that it has had a perfect safety record.

The reason Robert Moses gave for turning down Walter O'Malley's request to build a new Ebbetts Field in Brooklyn where Atlantic Center is now— O'Malley offered to pay all building costs and needed help only in acquiring the land, which was owned by the city—was that Moses felt a parking garage would be more suitable in that location, and he suggested that the Dodgers move to Queens.

What do the streets named Marcy, Tomkins, Lewis, Throop, and Yates in Bedford-Stuyvesant have in common? They are the names of former governors of New York State.

In the nineteenth century, the fact that New York owned the rights to the East River (Brooklyn's ownership stopped at the shoreline) encouraged the authorities there to think of trying to collect a fee from not only the owners of the ferries operating from Brooklyn to New York, but also Brooklynites who rowed across the East River in their own boats.

In a survey of houses of worship in Brooklyn in the 1890s, it was revealed that most were Catholic (sixty-three churches), followed by Protestant Episcopal (forty-five churches) and Presbyterian (thirty-three churches). There were ten synagogues.

In 1908, a large crowd estimated to be over twenty-five thousand assembled to watch the burning of the Park Theater on Fulton Street in Downtown Brooklyn. Fortunately, it occurred in the late afternoon after the matinee audience had left the theater, and no one was injured. Here is a somewhat humorous sidelight reported by the *NY Times*: "Unaware that flames were already consuming the roof, the box office on the first floor was still selling tickets for the evening performance."

The Brooklyn Navy Yard was not the only place in Brooklyn that produced warships. During both world wars, the Atlantic Basin Iron Works in Red Hook not only repaired and serviced navy ships but also made them.

During the Civil War, the women in the congregation of the Clinton Avenue Congregational Church did more than their duty. For Brooklyn's 28th Regiment, they made 1,500 yards of bandages.

The Soldiers and Sailors Memorial Arch at the entrance to Prospect Park, Brooklyn, attracted national attention when it was built. When its cornerstone was laid in 1889, one of the main speakers was General William T. Sherman, and when the unveiling took place three years later, President Grover Cleveland was in attendance.

During the American Revolution, many Tories in Brooklyn, as well as Tories from New York who rowed over, would celebrate the anniversary of King George III's coronation with a special fish dinner and fireworks at the King's Head Tavern located at what is now the corner of Main Street and Old Fulton Street in DUMBO. In the invitation to the 1780 celebration was a line that said, "It is expected that no rebel will approach nearer than Flatbush wood."

Did you know that the original proposal for the Parade Ground in Prospect Park located it in East New York?

For years after a new St. Ann's Protestant Episcopal Church was built in 1874 at the corner of Clinton Street and Livingston Street, it was called St. Ann's on the Heights in order to differentiate it from the church's previous building on Sands Street in what is now DUMBO.

I wonder how many of those who enter the Promenade through the entrance at the end of Pierrepont Street know that at the children's playground to the left is where the home of Henry E. Pierrepont once stood, which some say may have been the most opulent mansion in all of Brooklyn. It was torn down in 1947 during the construction of the BQE and the Promenade.

When Deno's Wonder Wheel was built at Coney Island in 1920, the construction material was 100 percent Bethlehem Steel hand-forged right on the spot.

As late as 1830, there was corn still being grown on Montague Street in Brooklyn Heights.

Considering that the Brooklyn Dodgers had a reputation for ineptness in many of its years, it is a little surprising to learn that the team won the National League pennant no less than six times before the team left in 1957. If you count the times it won under other names like the Robins, Superbas, and Bridegrooms, the total becomes eleven.

So rife was the area around the Brooklyn Navy Yard in the 1920s with prostitution, gambling, and crime that the US Navy stationed a permanent Shore

Patrol unit on Sands Street to prevent US sailors from entering.

Abraham & Straus notwithstanding, for years, the number 1 department store in Downtown Brooklyn was Martin's across the street, which catered to the affluent and, in the 1940s, according to the *New York Times*, sold more wedding dresses than any other retail outlet in the United States.

According to one source, the first Jewish man in Williamsburg was a man named Adolph Baker.

In case you didn't know, Maimonides—for whom Maimonides Medical Center in Bensonhurst was named—was a twelfth-century philosopher who established the concept of medicine as a science and authored ten books that set the foundation of modern medicine and the training of physicians.

From 1872 when it opened its factory in Greenpoint to 1956 when it relocated to Wilkes-Barre, Pennsylvania, an important employer in Brooklyn was the Eberhard-Faber Co. Not only was it the nation's number 1 pencil manufacturer, but it also pioneered in hiring women for factory work at a time most females were employed as domestics.

Did you ever wonder how DUMBO came to be called DUMBO (Down Under the Manhattan Bridge Overpass)? According to one account, this came about in 1978 when a group of artists living there deliberately dreamed up the name to sound silly and unattractive in order to discourage real-estate interests from wanting to develop the area.

Did you know that the last two years the Dodgers were in Brooklyn, they played some of their games in the Roosevelt Stadium in Jersey City?

When New York City delisted Red Hook Lane as a street last year, there was still one house standing on it.

When the original Brooklyn Academy of Music was built in 1859, it was the largest public meeting place in the city.

Yes, Brooklyn had a Tompkins Park just as New York does. Located in Bedford-Stuyvesant, it was originally designed in the 1870s by Frederick Law Olmsted and Calvert Vaux, who were responsible for Prospect Park. Even though its official name was changed in 1985 to Herbert Von King Park in honor of a prominent local civic leader, many people still call it Tompkins Park.

One of the more successful patent medicine manufacturers in the United States in the late nineteenth century and early twentieth century was a Brooklyn company that made Lydia Pinkham's Liver Pills, which were "guaranteed to cure constipation, biliousness, and toxicity."

In founding Pratt Institute in Brooklyn, Charles Pratt used the format Peter Cooper had used in his founding of Cooper Union as his major guideline.

When the Dreamland Amusement Park at Coney Island burned down in 1911, most of the city's newspapers ignored the story.

Did you know that Brownsville was an early home of the Socialist Labor Movement?

If you want to know where in Brooklyn the largest collection of mature trees in New York City is, according to the Brooklyn Botanic Garden, it is in Green-Wood Cemetery. Even before Green-Wood participated in the Million Trees NYC program in 2008, Green-Wood had 7,540 trees. It added several hundred trees, including 115 different oaks. All in all, according to the Brooklyn Botanic Garden, Green-Wood Cemetery has the largest collection of mature trees in New York City.

If you want to know when gaslights were introduced in Brooklyn, the year was 1848.

You might wonder how many old-timers in Brooklyn Heights like myself remember the dry cleaner's that was once located on Clinton Street between Joralemon and Remsen Streets, which was one of the last in the city to use naphtha as a cleaning agent and which had posted on a wall a 1928 letter from Calvin Coolidge sent from the White House, saying how satisfied he was with the coat the establishment had cleaned for him.

If those Brooklynites shopping on Fulton Street in Downtown Brooklyn had looked up one morning on September 17, 1911, they would have seen history in the making. Flying above the street was the first aviator to complete a transcontinental flight—Calbreath Rodgers, who had taken off a few minutes earlier from Sheepshead Bay and who landed in Pasadena, California, almost three months later on December 10, 1911. Unable to fly at night (there were no lights then to guide him), he had made more than seventy stops along the way to refuel and make repairs. His actual flying time was eighty-two hours.

Did you know that there was a landmark police precinct stationhouse in Brooklyn whose building was constructed in 1898 to resemble a medieval castle? It was the 20th Police Precinct Station House and Stable—later the 83rd Precinct Station House—and it is located at 120 Wilson Avenue in Bushwick.

Ironically, Robert Moses—who, more than anyone else, transformed New York into an "automobile" city with his roadways, tunnels, and bridges—never had a driver's license and, according to some, did not know how to drive.

The historians at Plymouth Church of the Pilgrims (then Plymouth Church) can tell you exactly where Lincoln sat when he came to Brooklyn in 1860 to hear Reverend Henry Ward Beecher speak, but they cannot tell you where he sat when he came two weeks later. This is because he sat in a numbered pew the first time; the second time, he was in the balcony where the seats are not numbered.

In a review of the acclaimed novel *Call It Sleep* by Henry Roth, a writer from Brownsville, a book critic wrote, "This book is to Brownsville what *Moby Dick* is to Nantucket."

Before World War II, Horn and Hardart, the Automat self-service restaurant chain, was selling its popular macaroni-and-cheese dish for all of five cents!

I wonder how many people know that Gateway National Park, which spreads out over thirty thousand acres in Brooklyn, Queens, Staten Island, and Sandy Hook, has the honor of being the first national urban park in the United States?

Although Coney Island Creek, which once divided Coney Island from the rest of Brooklyn, is now filled in, there was a time not so long ago when the city of New York proposed to widen it so it could accommodate ships.

Another major product first manufactured in Brooklyn was Mack Trucks. It started out in the year 1909 as the Mack Brothers Co. and, in the beginning, produced not only trucks but buses and trolley buses as well.

In 1896 when Brooklyn's trolley workers went on strike, there was so much fighting between them and the trolley company's officials that the mayor of Brooklyn had to call out the Seventh Regiment to maintain order.

If you ever wondered how Diamond Jim Brady—who summered at Coney Island in the Gay Nineties—made the money to finance his jewelry purchases, the answer is that he was the chief salesman for the Pressed Steel Car Co., the leading manufacturer of passenger railroad cars in the United States.

The career of James Creighton, the pitcher for the Brooklyn Excelsiors who was baseball's first superstar and the nation's first ballplayer to get paid (they were all amateur players up to then), didn't last very long. Two years after he signed his contract in 1860, he collapsed in the middle of a ballgame and died at the age of twenty-nine.

In the 1860s, in order to preserve the tranquility and contemplative atmosphere of Green-Wood Cemetery, signs were posted advising those visitors who drove carriages through the cemetery to "drive slow."

Did you know that Mount Prospect Park, which lies between the Brooklyn Public Library and the Brooklyn Botanic Garden on Eastern Parkway, was originally not a park, but the location of Brooklyn's first major reservoir?

One of the many well-known American companies that started out in Brooklyn was Benjamin Moore Paint. In 1883, it built its first factory at 231 Front Street in Vinegar Hill.

In 1928, when the Leverich Towers in Brooklyn Heights opened, the four towers located at the corners of its roof—which gave the hotel its name—were illuminated by spotlights at night. EVERICHTowers Hotel on Clark St opened the four towers at each corner which gavethei name to thehotelend from whichitgot its name was

In 1911, the *Handbook of the Women's Municipal League* published an article titled "The Working Girls of Coney Island," which revealed that the average wage of the women who worked there was $1.00 to $1.50 per day. Wages ranged from $3 per week (toilet tending) to $13 per week (experienced cashiers).

The original Brooklyn Academy of Music on Montague Street was not the only venue for performances by noted American actors of the late nineteenth century. Another Brooklyn theater that presented first-class plays was the Park Theater located on Fulton Street facing Brooklyn's City Hall (now Borough Hall). Among those who trod the boards there were matinee idols of the day, like Edwin Booth and Maurice Barrymore.

In colonial days, there were accidents on the horsepower ferryboats just as there was in the twenty-first century when a Staten Island ferry crashed. A newspaper account from 1775 noted that a ferry crossing the East River from Brooklyn overturned, causing the death through drowning of "one man and eight fat cows."

If you want to know where the Lesbian Herstory Archives is located, the address is 484 Fourteenth Street in Park Slope.

Contrary to the reputation the neighborhood of Bedford had in the mid-1900s when it was linked to the Stuyvesant neighborhood, a century before it was considered to be one of the elite places to live in Brooklyn, with affluent residents, a network of parks and clubs, and excellent schools such as Boys High School and Girls High School.

The first electric trolley line within Kings County was the one that started operating between Queens and East New York in 1887.

Austin Corbin, the financier who built the elegant Manhattan Beach Hotel in the late 1800s, made no bones about being an anti-Semite. In an interview with the *New York Times*, he explained that the reason he had a fence around the hotel and Pinkerton guards was to keep out Jews and others he thought undesirable. "As a class," he said blatantly, "Jews have made themselves offensive to those who patronize my hotel and I will leave nothing undone to get rid of them."

Brooklyn saw its first elevated train line in 1885. It ran from the Brooklyn Bridge to Broadway.

One of the features of the now-gone Brighton Bath, Beach, and Racquet Club was that its lifeguards—unusual for the time—were women.

As some of my readers informed me when I noted in a recent column that there were only two Parkways in Brooklyn, I was off the mark by more than half a dozen, failing to include Belt Parkway, Bay Ridge Parkway, Rockaway Beach Parkway, etc.

At one point after World War II, a circuit of Warner Brothers–named Fabian Theaters owned three of Downtown Brooklyn's biggest theaters—the Paramount, the Fox, and the Strand.

What most people don't know about Kingsborough Community College is that it maintains the world's largest website on lighthouses.

After emerging from a ride on Coney Island's Cyclone roller coaster, Charles Lindbergh said it was "more thrilling" than his record-breaking solo flight across the Atlantic Ocean.

Did you know that the Brooklyn Museum on Eastern Parkway started out in the early nineteenth century as a library in Brooklyn Heights designed to "shield young men from evil associations and encourage their improvement during leisure hours"?

One source says the apartment that Douglas Fairbanks and Mary Pickford lived in when making films at Brooklyn's Vitagraph Studios was on Ocean Parkway facing Prospect Park. Supposedly, its bathtub had gold faucets.

In the nation's first census taken in 1790, it was recorded that slightly more than six hundred Brooklyn families owned slaves, a higher percentage than that of any other county in New York State.

Brooklyn's first "acquisition" took place in 1816 when Downtown Brooklyn was officially added to its boundaries.

In the late nineteenth century, a company called the Boynton Bicycle Railroad Co. attempted to bring monorail transportation to Brooklyn. Based on patents of inventor Eben Boynton, who for years had been promoting a monorail system for all of Long Island, it built about a mile and a half of overhead track over an old railroad line from Gravesend to Coney Island and in 1889 ran an experimental train over it consisting of an engine and a passenger car containing some one hundred dignitaries and invited guests, the propulsion coming from a gigantic wheel some eight feet in diameter powered by steam. Unfortunately for the company, it could not get financing to go further, and all that remains of the Boynton Bicycle Railroad Co. are vestiges of where the experiment took place.

When the city's ambulance service started up in Brooklyn in the late nineteenth century, it was for indigents only. To get an ambulance, one had to schedule it through the Bureau of Charities.

Regarding the new fruit stand in front of the St. George Hotel entrance on Henry Street, one of my most faithful readers reminds me (thanks, EW) that in the 1970s there was a farmer who sold vegetables from a horse-drawn wagon he parked regularly in front of the Mansion House apartment complex on Hicks Street.

Another interesting character buried in Green-Wood Cemetery was Peter Relyea, an undertaker who was in charge of the funeral procession of Abraham Lincoln as it passed through New York on its way to the late president's final resting place in Springfield, Illinois. For his services, including constructing the catafalque that carried the coffin (he worked day and night to complete it on time), he was paid $9,000.

The baseball team that Brooklyn had in the big leagues had many names before it was known as the Dodgers. One of these names, along with the Superbas and the Bridegrooms, was simply the Brooklyn Baseball Club, and among its players were three Hall of Famers—Ned Hanlon, a famous manager in the late nineteenth century; Wee Willie Keeler, one of the game's greatest hitters; and Hughie Jennings, an outstanding shortstop in the early days.

According to the *AIA Guide to New York City*, the classic guide to New York architecture, the buildings of Packer Collegiate resemble "a British Victorian businessman's Gothic castle."

Although John Ericsson is usually the one given credit for the *Monitor*, the world's first iron-clad warship, he was really only the ship's designer. The man who actually built it at the Continental Iron Works in Greenpoint in 1862 was Thomas E. Rowland.

Did you know that there is an exhibit at the New York Aquarium at Coney Island that children are allowed to touch? It's the one containing the horseshoe crabs.

You will find the name of Vincenzio Capone, Al Capone's brother, in the anti-crime files of the US government, but not as a gangster as you might suspect. Rather, Vincenzio changed his name in his adult life and became a federal agent assigned to track down bootleggers during Prohibition. Under the name of "Two-Gun Hart," he became almost as widely publicized as his brother.

Did you know that the finest racing drivers in the nation—Louis Chevrolet, Eddie Rickenbacker, and Barney Oldfield—competed for prizes in Brooklyn in World War I days when a man named Harry Harkness converted the Sheepshead Bay Racetrack to automobile racing after the New York State Legislature banned horseracing in 1910?

Many of the neighborhoods in New Utrecht, one of Brooklyn's original six towns, still survive, such as Bay Ridge, Fort Hamilton, Dyker Heights, Boro Park, Bath Beach, and parts of Bensonhurst. However, some of the other neighborhoods, like Blythebourne, Lefferts Park, and Van Pelt Manor, are little more than a memory.

Yes, it's true. When you get off the subway at Stillwell Avenue, the Nathan's Famous across Surf Avenue is the original Nathan's Famous that opened in 1916 and was the beginning of the chain that now includes more than one thousand Nathan's Famous outlets.

The baseball team that Brooklyn had in the big leagues had many names before it was known as the Dodgers. One of these names, along with the Superbas and the Bridegrooms, was simply the Brooklyn Baseball Club. Among its players were three Hall of Famers—Ned Hanlon, a famous manager in the late nineteenth century; Wee Willie Keeler, one of the game's greatest hitters; and Hughie Jennings, an outstanding shortstop in the early days.

According to the *AIA Guide to New York City*, the classic guide to New York architecture, the buildings of Packer Collegiate resemble "a British Victorian businessman's Gothic castle."

In the beginning, it cost five cents to walk over the Brooklyn Bridge.

Five years before night games came to the big leagues in 1935, Dexter Park in Queens—home to the semipro teams like the Brooklyn Bushwicks and teams from the Negro leagues—was electrified.

Although it is widely known that Henry Ward Beecher auctioned off a young black girl from his

Plymouth Church pulpit to demonstrate the evils of slavery, not so well known is that this was only the first of three such auctions he eventually staged.

Did you know the Brooklyn Botanic Garden has a fragrance section where the descriptions of the flowers and herbs are printed in Braille?

There is some evidence that the house at 64 Popular Street in Brooklyn Heights, which dates back to 1834, was built by Walt Whitman and his father.

Although the 11,500 prisoners imprisoned in the British prison ships in Wallabout Bay during the American Revolution were from all over—with some even picked up on the high seas by the British Navy—most were Continental Army soldiers captured during the Battle of Brooklyn.

Before people began to think seriously about a bridge over the East River linking Brooklyn and Manhattan, various proposals were put forth. Some were sensible, like having a tunnel, and others were in the realm of science fiction, like damming up the East River and erecting a dike that would have a drawbridge in the middle to allow vessels through and boulevards on each side for pedestrians and carriages.

We not only know the name of the Hessian soldier who, during the American Revolution, scratched his name (Georg Ernst Toepfer) on the pane of the window of the Bennett house at the southeast corner of Kings Highway and East Twenty-Second Street where he was quartered, but we also know his rank (Capt. Reg: de Dittfourth).

According to one source, it was Seth Low—the only man to have been mayor of both Brooklyn (before the Consolidation) and Greater New York (after the Consolidation)—who, in a Decoration Day speech at Green-Wood Cemetery, first proposed what became the Soldiers and Sailors Monument at Grand Army Plaza.

Although the Whitney family in 1920 donated 220,000 acres of land to establish a park that became Maine Park (land was also donated by Alfred T. White and Frederick Pratt), it took the Parks Department more than a decade to open it up to the public.

He was a Brooklyn physician named Frederick Cook, and he was the most controversial figure in Arctic exploration. He claimed to have been the first man to ascend Mount Whitney and to have stood on the North Pole fifteen days before Robert Peary did. He also claimed that it was Peary's lies that robbed him of the credit for his achievements. A five-year prison term for being involved in a fraudulent oil scheme didn't help his cause much, even though later he did get a presidential pardon from FDR. He died uncredited in 1940, although supporters continue to plead his case.

It didn't take long for the Apprentices Library that Lafayette dedicated in 1825 to outgrow its space. Within ten years, it had to move to a larger space on Washington Street in Clinton Hill.

For some Brooklynites, the allegiance to England lasted a long time after England was decisively beaten in the American Revolution. As late as the first quarter of the nineteenth century, the King's Colors were seen hanging in a tavern in Flatbush.

According to one account, it was Seth Low, one-time mayor of both Brooklyn and later Greater New York, who suggested in a Decoration Day speech at Green-Wood Cemetery building the Soldiers and Sailors Monument that now stands at the entrance to Grand Army Plaza.

When the Municipal Baths in Coney Island were at the corner of Surf Avenue and Fifth Street, you could rent a towel for five cents or ten cents, depending on the size you wanted.

When in the early 1900s the Tomkins Congregational Church merged with the Flatbush Congregational Church, the combined number of members—some 2,400—made it the largest Congregational Church in the United States.

Did you know that Willard Mullin modeled his well-known caricature of "Der Bum" after the famous circus clown Emmett Kelly?

Marty Markowitz, the most vociferous and energetic borough president Brooklyn ever had, started his annual summer concerts at Coney Island when he was a state senator.

In this historic baseball game, which took place in 1926 when the Brooklyn Dodgers were the Brooklyn Robins, the home team ended up with three men on one base (third base) in what has been described as the most boneheaded play in big-league baseball. The Brooklyn players were Dazzy Vance, Chick Fewster, and Babe Herman.

The four hundred lights used over the ring where sports history had its first heavyweight boxing championship at night at the Coney Island Athletic Club in 1899 were so hot that they singed the hair of the two boxers, James J. Jeffries and Sailor Tom Sharkey.

No one knows for sure how many contract killings were carried out by the gangster members of Brooklyn's Murder Inc. Estimates run from four hundred to one thousand.

It was *Hearst* columnist Westbrook Pegler who coined the phrase "The Daffiness Boys" to describe the Brooklyn Dodgers.

Supposedly, when you had a job at Abraham and Straus (now Macy's), you had a job for life and would never be fired.

Did you know that Junior's Restaurant started out as a sandwich shop named Enduro?

At one point, when it was allowed, the owner of the Baltimore Orioles owned the team that later became the Brooklyn Dodgers.

You would think the British bank Barclays paid $200 million to put its name on Brooklyn's indoor sports arena to promote its consumer business in the United States, but actually, it does not have a branch or even an ATM outlet here.

There was a reason that Brooklyn's major-league ball team was once called the Bridegrooms. Six of its players were engaged to be married.

There is a fleeting reference to Brooklyn in the Sherlock Holmes story "The Case of the Norwood Builder" when Holmes noted that Watson had an unframed portrait of Henry Ward Beecher, Brooklyn's famous minister, on the wall where he kept his books,.

Ebbets Field, where the Dodgers played, may have been the smallest home-team baseball field in the major leagues, but it was the first "modern" ball field and was the model of those that were built later.